How to Make
Your Baby an
Internet Celebrity

How to Make Your Baby an Internet Celebrity

GUIDING YOUR CHILD TO SUCCESS AND FULFILLMENT

by Rick Chillot

with photography by
Dustin Fenstermacher

QUIRK
BOOKS

Disclaimer: No babies, human or otherwise, or other living creatures aside from the book designer and copy editor were harmed in the making of this book. The author and publisher do not condone placing any baby or person in harm's way even for a laugh or a quick buck. Babies are our future!

Library of Congress Cataloging in Publication Number: 2013957074

ISBN: 978-1-59474-739-7

Printed in China
Typeset in Helvetica
Book design by Amanda Richmond
Photo doodles by Doogie Horner
Production management by John J. McGurk

Quirk Books
215 Church Street
Philadelphia, PA 19106
quirkbooks.com

10 9 8 7 6 5 4 3 2 1

Contents

If Destiny Is Fussy, Burp It

Congratulations on your new baby! Welcome to the world of midnight feedings, sunrise wake-up calls, doctor's visits, routine vaccinations, infant CPR lessons, American Sign Language flash cards, art appreciation classes, stroller maintenance workshops, and other exciting responsibilities.

But as a loving and responsible parent, you have one obligation that's far more important than any of those others: making your baby an Internet celebrity.

Most readers will find the reasons for doing this to be obvious, perhaps insultingly so, and can skip ahead to Chapter 1. But for those of you with even the slightest bit of skepticism or concern, let's connect a few dots. Raising children in the twenty-first century is unlike anything your parents or grandparents experienced, and the stakes could not be higher. Consider the world your child is going to inherit: scarce jobs, fierce competition, dwindling opportunities. Experts tell us that the global economy will worsen while household appliances will get smarter. By the time your child is twenty-one years old and ready to enter the workforce, all of her job interviews will be conducted by Roombas. If she's lucky, she'll be one of thousands of equally qualified candidates vying for a slice of the vocational pie. More likely, she'll have to compete with millions of rivals from foreign nations who learned to read at the age of two and learned to speak while still in the womb.

As you can see, your baby was born behind the eight ball, and you'd better hurry before the pool cue of fate lines up a bank shot into the corner pocket of oblivion. For your grandparents and great-grandparents, success was a reward for working hard and keeping their noses to the grindstone, but those days are over. In the new global economy, there are simply too many noses— roughly 6.3 noses for every grindstone, with more emerging every day. Besides, do you even know what a grindstone is? Does it sound like something you'd want your child's nose pressed against? You know it's probably covered in germs.

So what are you and your new baby going to do? In these crucial early months, too many parents waste time loafing around, waiting for the baby to congeal into something of substance like a Jell-O mold in a cluttered refrigerator. But if your child waits until preschool or kindergarten (or, worse, elementary school) to "discover" his talents and passions, he'll be too late. The time to establish your child's platform and brand identity is *now*, while all the other babies are napping twelve to sixteen hours a day. And the easiest way to establish your child's future persona—to put him so far in front of his age cohort that he'll be driving a Bugatti to accept his Nobel Prize on the moon while his peers are picking their noses in line at the DMV—is to turn your baby into an Internet celebrity.

Now, I've heard all the standard concerns and reservations, like "Won't becoming famous turn my sweet Thumbelina into a narcissistic sociopathic jerk?" And it's true, that is a common consequence of traditional fame. However, you need to remember that we are talking about *Internet* fame, a much safer and healthier alternative. Consider:

Your baby, with regular fame

Must spend hours on stage or on a movie or TV set

Acting, dancing, or other talent may be necessary

Will eventually wrest control of own career and/or turn to a life of petty crime out of resentment

Money will be eaten up by agents, stylists, managers, directors, lawyers, and publicists

Your baby, with Internet fame

Need only spend minutes per day in front of a webcam or smartphone

Only basic mundane behavior required: breathing, crying, pooping, giggling, eating, pooping again, etc.

Won't notice that she's famous, and has no say in it anyway

All money goes to the baby's 529 college savings account

Of course you'll want to think long and hard about whether this is the right course of action for your baby. But you must ignore that instinct, because there's no time to waste! Your baby's most valuable asset—cuteness—is diminishing by the day. So forget about five-year plans, acting classes, or a musical-based secondary school like they have on *Glee*. If you really want to finance the best life possible for your little one, you've got to act *now*, while little Blair or Gregg is well worth looking at. In fact, the most responsible parents will begin shaping their child's Web persona at conception.

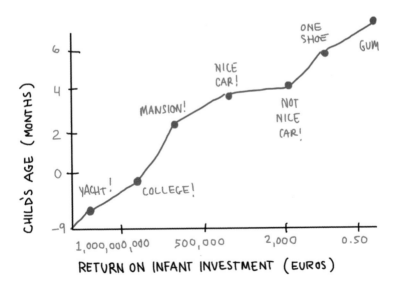

-9 to 0 months:

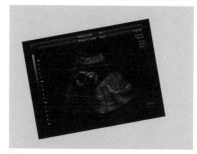

Start sending press releases; post short clips to create buzz.

0 to 3 months:

"Human blob" stage. Cuteness on the rise. Begin video career.

3 to 12 months:

Peak cuteness reached. Maximal revenue opportunities.

12 months-plus:

Washed up. No visual appeal left. File for public assistance if needed.

Still not convinced? Try this exercise. Set down this book, walk over to the bassinet, and take a good, long look at your child. Now what do you see?

Do you see a helpless, chubby-cheeked protohuman about to sink into a lifetime of warm mediocrity like a meatball dropped into a pot of store-bought pasta sauce? I doubt it.

More likely you see someone truly remarkable, someone blessed with extraordinary gifts and tremendous potential. I bet you see a baby who is (1) simply the best, (2) better than all the rest, and (3) better than anyone, anyone you've ever met. I bet you want your baby to have every advantage life can offer. And if you're that type of parent, it's damn well time you started acting like it.

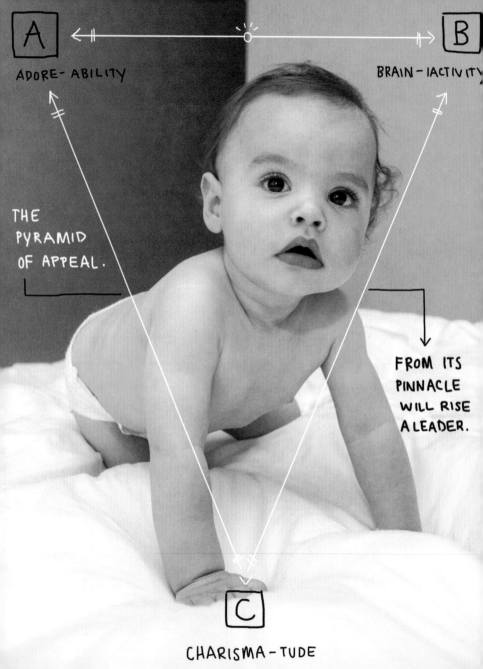

CHAPTER 1

Baby Steps toward Colossal Success

Let's begin our journey with a key question that every responsible parent *must* ask: Is my baby one of the good ones—cute, smart, charismatic, relatively drool-free? Or is my baby one of the *awe-inspiring* ones, the type whose ineffable magnetism could inspire a mystery cult or heal a rift between nations?

The ABC Method: Find Out How Oddly Appealing Your Baby Really Is

Fortunately, scientists somewhere have determined probably that the attractiveness of all babies can be quantified by ranking them on a scale of 1 to 5 along three independent axes. All you have to do is rate your child according to the following standards. Be honest!

ADORE-ABILITY:
HOW SUPERCUTE IS THIS BABY?

1. You can't win them all, right?

2. If by cute, you mean vaguely lizardlike, then very!

3. If the local TV station had a baby newsroom, this baby could be . . . not the anchor, no, but maybe the weekend anchor, or the weatherbaby.

4. Planned Parenthood has affirmed that if enough people get a look at this baby, nobody will use birth control ever again.

5. When other babies meet this baby, they get jealous and immediately develop eating disorders.

BRAIN-IACTIVITY:
HOW CLEVER IS THIS BABY?

1. Admittedly, she got lost on the way out of the womb.

2. On her second day of life, she traded her blanket and booties with another baby for a bag of "magic beans."

3. She can already count to ten, though not with words anyone can understand.

4. She is capable of using simple tools and comprehending a few dozen words; she has roughly the intellect of an adolescent chimpanzee.

5. She speaks in complete sentences, all of them condescending.

CHARISMA-TUDE:
HOW MUCH PERSONALITY, CHARM, OR "'TUDE" DOES THIS BABY OOZE?

1. He repels people like a reverse magnet.

2. He is often mistaken for a pile of small stones.

3. Think beige. Beige is a nice color, right? I mean, it's not *un*pleasant.

4. This is the kind of baby you find yourself constantly saying "Oh no you di'n't!" to (rhetorically).

5. Meet this baby, and you'll know what it felt like to give frankincense to baby Jesus (and wish it had been gold).

The best way to find your baby's ABC score is to set up a focus group: Allow a few dozen strangers to spend some time with the infant and then have them rate her in each category. (Don't offer to pay them; when they get a look at your child, *they* will offer to pay *you*. Agree.) Listen to their feedback, rate the kid as best you can, and find her spot on the chart below.

THE ABC RATING SYSTEM:
Where does your child fit in?

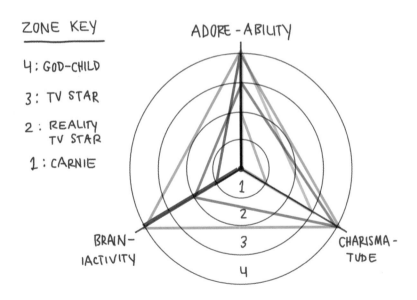

ZONE KEY

4 : GOD-CHILD

3 : TV STAR

2 : REALITY
     TV STAR

1 : CARNIE

ADORE-ABILITY

BRAIN-
IACTIVITY

CHARISMA-
TUDE

EXAMPLES

GERBER BABY   A4, B1, C0

PRINCE GEORGE OF CAMBRIDGE   A2, B0, C1

AVERAGE MUPPET BABY   A4, B2, C4

BABY DUCKLING   A4, B0, C3

STAR CHILD, 2001: A SPACE ODYSSEY   A0, B4, C0

SUCCESS BABY   A4, B4, C4

The highest zone your baby reaches on the chart will in turn determine how much success you'll have origami-ing him into a beloved worldwide media personality. Here's what the zones mean:

ZONE 4: Ka-ching! Your baby might as well be pooping out gold coins into a platinum diaper that's coated with baby powder made from ground-up pearls. You'll be changing diapers all the way to the bank! But wash your hands first.

ZONE 3: You've got a diamond in the rough here, ready to cut and polish. So prepare to roll up your sleeves and stick one of those weird jeweler's thingies in your eye. Also know that one wrong move will irreversibly ruin this precious gem forever.

ZONE 2: You've got a tough row to hoe. It can be hard to get people interested in something this bland. On the other hand, manila envelopes are pretty bland, and they're among the most popular office supplies. So there's hope.

ZONE 1: Congratulations! You seem to have some kind of aberrant baby who possesses one or more qualities that rate below the threshold of what the squares call "normal." But that's good! People are fascinated by the exotic and strange, which is why pugs are such popular pets.

ZONE 4

ZONE 1

Persona Infanta:
Baby Types

Good job, parent! You've pinpointed your baby's primary strengths and weaknesses. Next, it's time to up the ante by slotting that child into the proper toaster of transformation, whence he'll pop up with a crispy, buttery new identity.

Think of babies as blank slates awaiting a more compelling narrative. But just as the witness protection program tries not to place Jersey mobsters into small Amish communities, some assignments make more sense than others. Use this list to match your tiny tot with the perfect persona or character type—what psychologist Carl Jung called an "archetype"—a persona that will really pop on camera and leave your fellow parents in the dust. When done correctly, this persona will establish a "brand identity" that leads to a lucrative career later in life.

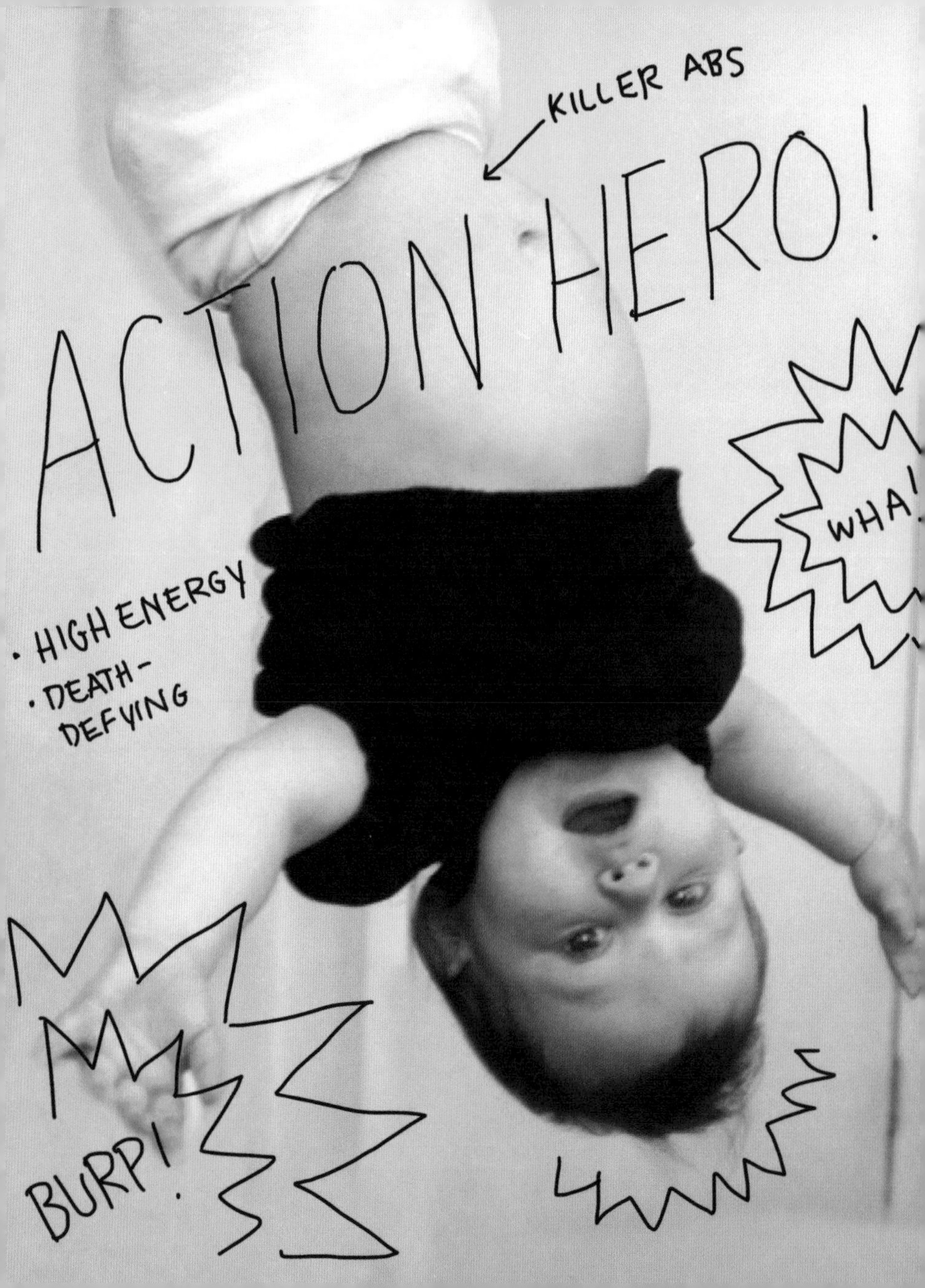
KILLER ABS
ACTION HERO!
WHA!
· HIGH ENERGY
· DEATH-DEFYING
BURP!

IS YOUR BABY AN ACTION HERO?

- Did your baby learn to vault before she could crawl?

- Did she have to fight off a gang of ninjas who were waiting just outside the uterus?

- Is Danger this baby's middle name, even though you clearly put "Mandy" on the birth certificate?

Raising the Action Hero: This is a baby who likes to move, so make sure you're in top shape or you're going to be left behind like a used diaper. To slow her down, try tying weights to her legs, or perhaps rearrange the furniture in the nursery into a kind of obstacle course. Maybe hire a nanny who's a failed Olympic decathlete.

Filming the Action Hero: You'll want a camera with a wide-angle lens, which will capture the true cinematic glory of a baby who can scale a bookcase or jump from a careening tricycle before it crashes. Consider inventing a catchphrase that you can display on the screen when the baby completes a stunt: "I'm getting too old for this crap" or "I picked the wrong day to start weaning."

Future career options: Navy SEAL, kung fu sensei, treasure hunter who plays by her own rules

IS YOUR BABY AN INTELLECTUAL?

- Did this baby figure out, at a very early age, that you did not in fact have his nose?

- Has this baby added footnotes and annotations to his copy of *Pat the Bunny*?

- Has this baby ever replicated the periodic table of elements using blocks and crayons? *With* lanthanides and actinides?

Raising the Intellectual Baby: Stimulate your brainiac's intellect every day. Dress up your family as a mariachi band, serve breakfast on the deck of a tall ship, spend a day observing weasels in the wild . . . don't give those brain cells a moment to stop growing.

Filming the Intellectual Baby: It's not good enough to hand this baby a book or a microscope and film the results. Anyone can look smart with the right accouterments, even Erwin Schrödinger, whose theory of quantum mechanics was ridiculed until he added an umlaut to his name. Try replicating intelligence tests used on chimps in captivity, such as matching shapes, remembering complex commands, or figuring out how to roller-skate. Use a clipboard to add verisimilitude.

Future career options: CEO of Mensa; professor whose class consists solely of other professors; inventor of his own career

Gourmand
BON APPÉTIT!
FOOD
FOOD
CAUTION!
FOOD INTAKE PORT
FOOD
FOOD
FOOD
FOOD

IS YOUR BABY A GOURMAND?

- If breast-fed, does this baby have a marked preference for one side over the other?

- If bottle-fed, does she refuse feedings unless the formula is infused with truffle oil, coconut water, or lemongrass?

- Does the baby insist on riding in a Whole Foods shopping cart even when you're at Bottom Dollar Food?

Raising the Gourmand Baby: Don't listen to critics who are repulsed by your child's tendency to shove her entire face into a bowl of pabulum and not come up for air until every morsel has been hoovered into her voracious maw. You've birthed a food enthusiast! Someday she could go from food blogger to celebrity chef to just plain celebrity!

Filming the Gourmand Baby: Plop the kid down in front of a bowl of supermarket-brand strained squash and film the tantrum that occurs because it's not an heirloom variety hand-harvested by Shakers. Alternately, let her go to town on a big trough of something she *does* like. It worked for Hogbaby, darling of the "Cute Baby/Repulsive Behavior" YouTube channel.

Future career options: Food Network show host, molecular gastronomist, four-star restaurateur

GOOF BALL

- ACCIDENT PRONE
- LOVES PUDDING
- ZANY EYES

PROPS:

A.　　B.　　C.

IS YOUR BABY A LOVABLE GOOFBALL?

- When your baby dumps a plate of mashed peas on people, do they admire the physical comedy instead of getting angry?

- Given free rein, would your baby be likely to wear his diaper on his head and his booties on his hands?

- Does the baby inspire comparison to Falstaff, Jughead Jones, or Kramer?

Raising the Lovable Goofball: It may appear that a baby who can't toddle across the floor without stepping in pudding or whose diaper is always getting tugged off by a mischievous puppy will never amount to much. But your Lovable Goofball is destined for better things. So try not to despair when he locks the keys inside his Little Tykes Pedal Car *yet again.*

Filming the Lovable Goofball: The universe rewards a buffoon. So keep the camera running as your child accidentally tumbles into a laundry basket full of socks . . . maybe there's a tasty cookie at the bottom? Yes, he dropped your car keys into a pile of dog poop. But wait—you've found the neighbor's missing purebred borzoi and now can claim the $50 reward!

Future career options: best friend to a millionaire who takes life too seriously, *Saturday Night Live* performer, U.S. senator

IS YOUR BABY A BADASS?

- Are you afraid to startle this baby for fear of having a Melissa & Doug Learning Toy thrown at your head?

- Does the baby have one or more tattoos that you can't account for?

- Has this baby ever smashed his bottle against the side of the crib and then threatened you with the plastic shards?

Raising the Badass Baby: It's too late to establish dominance over this little thug. The time to do that was in the womb (you never should have put up with all that kicking). Try to channel his aggression in a positive way, perhaps by letting him stomp on your aluminum cans before you recycle them. The important thing is that you start building wealth for this kid and lock it in a managed trust fund before he's big enough lose it all in a *The Fast and the Furious: Tokyo Drift*–style street race.

Filming the Badass Baby: Like a young Robert Mitchum, this infant will inevitably shove aside anyone who tries to impede his blitz to the top. So put him in his element: a room full of weak, cowering babies he can push around and show who's boss.

Future career options: crime syndicate kingpin, bomb defuser, champion land speed motorcycle racer

Sensitive Soul

SHHH!

- EASILY STARTLED
- CRIES INSTANTLY

POWERFUL TEAR DUCTS

SCARY THINGS:
- KITTENS
- AIR
- COTTON BALLS

IS YOUR BABY A SENSITIVE SOUL?

- Is your baby startled by her own breathing?

- Have you mounted a sway bar on the baby's crib so she won't be disturbed by the rotation of the earth?

- Are you unable to use your tube of sensitive skin cleansing cream because the sound of the cap opening will upset her tender disposition?

Raising the Sensitive Soul: Your primary task is to find out what it takes to keep this baby calm, so invest in deep-pile carpeting, blackout shades, a harpist, and anything else that will minimize potentially surprising phenomena. On the other hand . . .

Filming the Sensitive Soul: When the camera turns on, it's go time! Trigger her adorable look of shocked horror by any means necessary: bright lights, a puff of air through a drinking straw, a dissonant chord played on a mandolin, a wailing ghost, whatever. Just be prepared to use a different startler each time, because if this child starts getting used to anything, it's game over. And destiny's pop-o-matic does not allow re-rolling.

Future career options: poet, NPR commentator, Grammy-winning folk singer

FERAL

THICK FUR

FIRST WORD: AWOOOO!

RAZOR-SHARP FINGERNAILS

IS YOUR BABY FERAL?

- Do friends and family assume this baby was raised by wolves, even though they helped bring him home from the hospital?

- Does the baby have more hair than you?

- Does the baby mark territory by urinating around the edges of the room?

Raising the Feral Baby: In many ways this is an ideal situation. True, you'll have to trim those finger- and toenails daily. And then there's the howling. But Mother Nature, not you, will handle most of the parenting chores. Consider installing a cat flap in the back door, so the tyke can get out to the woods while you're busy booking appearances on Animal Planet.

Filming the Feral Baby: Animals and children are notoriously difficult to work with on camera. A kid who thinks he's an animal? Doubly challenging. Place the child in primal situations where his bestial instincts can take over: fighting with a butterfly for territory in the back yard, gnawing on an unfamiliar aunt, howling with the neighborhood dogs when the mailman passes by.

Future career options: exotic animal whisperer, werewolf, big game hunter

IS YOUR BABY ROYALTY?

- Does the baby refuse to eat caviar unless it's served on a spoon made from mother-of-pearl?

- Have you ever beheaded someone on the baby's behalf?

- Do peasant babies give this baby a tithe of their Cheerios?

Raising the Royal Baby: Even a baby born in a trailer park inhabited solely by hoboes might come into the world possessing a preference for luxury, whether it's velvet, ermine, or Ley .925 tequila. So feed her belief that she's superior. Consider adding a throne room to your house, get some half-witted relative to act as her valet, and for heaven's sake don't stop the coddling.

Filming the Royal Baby: Guess what? As far as everyone else is concerned, this deluded kid *isn't* superior to anything. And when that cold reality splashes into her smug, regal face, you've got the makings of a dramatic video. Document what happens when your becrowned, scepter-wielding would-be sovereign tries to assert authority at a day care, playground, or doctor's office. Will her innate desire to rule be enough to inspire fealty among the masses? It's literally the Battle of Hastings all over again.

Future career options: king or queen of somewhere or something

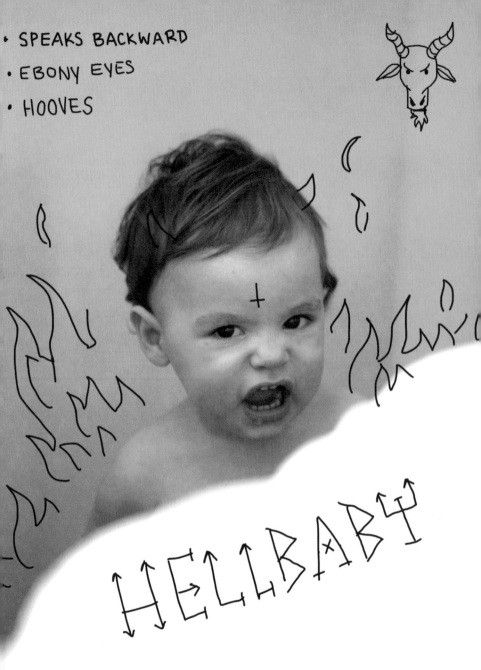

IS YOUR BABY A HELLBABY?

- Do you hear Latin chanting whenever this baby enters a room?

- Do mysterious and gruesome accidents befall anyone this baby doesn't like?

- Does the baby have a birthmark resembling an inverted star, a goat head, or the number 666?

Raising the Hellbaby: Sure, *you* know your child is an angelic spirit. But everyone else is convinced that she's the spawn of Lucifer—just because she is constantly screaming, has eyes like two deep pits of pure blackness . . . and then there was that 360-degree rotating head incident, which was probably just a trick of the light. So make that work *for* you—horror movies are popular, and your child could become the next Linda Blair, *Rosemary's Baby*, or *Damien: Omen II*.

Filming the Hellbaby: Stephen King has said that nothing is so frightening as what's behind the closed door. But Stephen King never met your kid! Eschew artsy, suspense-building filmmaker tricks like fade-ins or tracking shots. Just cut right to your baby and let that demonic rage tell its raw tale. If you can, capture her cursing, smacking somebody, or levitating. Don't be afraid to induce a tantrum by withholding toys or sprinkling her with holy water.

Future career options: cult leader, presidential candidate, banker

Q: HOW MANY BABIES CAN YOU FIND IN THIS PHOTO?

ANSWER: 12

3 IN DISHWASHER, 1 IN DISH SOAP, 2 UNDER BABY ON COUNTER, ALLIGATOR BABY ON SILL, YOUNG FLOWERS IN VASE, 1 IN YOUR HEART.

TRIPLETS!!!

IS YOUR BABY A TRIPLET?

- Is the baby often accompanied by two other babies who look exactly the same?

- Do you ever get the feeling, when feeding, dressing, or burping this baby, that you just did the exact same thing a few minutes earlier?

- Do you feel that this baby has as much charm, personality, and glamour as three ordinary babies?

Raising the Triplet: Okay, those days in the hospital were probably confusing, and you spent much of the time on medication. So think back. Are you *sure* you came home with just one baby? Because identical triplets are hard to tell apart, almost by definition. Is it possible you've been taking care of three different babies while thinking they were the same one? This would explain a lot, wouldn't it?

Filming the Triplet: If by dint of genetic lottery or overuse of fertility drugs you've been blessed with triplets, way to go! One baby is cute, two is cuter, but three is universally considered to be the optimum number of cuteness that the human brain can process. To wit:

HARVARD UNIVERSITY*
HUEY-DEWEY-LOUIE SCALE
OF NUMERICAL BABY CUTENESS

Number of babies	Observer reaction
1	Aww, cute.
2	They're so cute together!
3	OMG! So effing cute I can't stand it!!!
4	Now wait a minute . . .
5	Kinda horrifyin'.
6	WHAT IS GOING ON HERE?!
7	Please. Please, stop. Please. Please.
8	Freakish.

*Not affiliated with the real Harvard University.

If you're sure you *don't* have triplets, that's not a deal breaker. Careful placement of mirrors and/or the use of multiple takes and "green screen" photography can transform any charismatic infant into three. Or try hiring two extra babies of similar size and build (they all look pretty much the same for the first several months, right?).

Future career options: Cirque du Soleil performer(s), musical act, spokesmodel(s) for Triplemint Gum

Dressing and Garnishing: Make Your Baby Unrecognizable to Enhance Uniqueness

By now you're probably thinking, "Yes, this all makes so much sense . . . but is it enough? Can my baby really become famous and have the best possible life based solely on a careful assessment and exploitation of her characteristics, personality, and archetype? Is that all I need to do to ensure a bright financial future for my child?" The answer is: Have you noticed that there are more pages in this book? Geez, hold on to your haunches.

Perhaps your impatience is rooted in a fear that your baby isn't up to snuff. Hey, it happens. Not every baby is ready for inexplicable stardom right out of the box. Some babies are "real-life cute" rather than "Internet cute," which means they're actually kinda ordinary as far as the World Wide Web is concerned. Fortunately there's an easy way to disguise your baby's blandness: use a disguise.

Here's how: Take a look at your baby. A good, long look. Drink in this munchkin's adorableness until your every cell is quivering with parental affection. And then ask yourself: If this thing wasn't a baby, what could it be instead? What type of animal, vegetable, or rock does he most resemble? Next, locate or create a costume based on this observation. When your audience stops asking "What's the big deal about this baby?" and starts asking "Is that actually a baby?" you'll know you've hit pay dirt. As an example, consider Mini Prime Minister, whose resemblance to Winston Churchill resulted in a string of viral videos on YouTube's "Baby Political Theatre" channel. If those parents had given up just because their baby lacked mainstream cuteness, the world never would have enjoyed that famous "We shall fight them in the playgrounds" speech.

Here are some ideas to get you started.

When your audience stops asking "What's the big deal about this baby?" and starts asking "Is that actually a baby?" you'll know you've hit pay dirt.

If your baby is ...	Your baby could be styled to look like ...
Always waggling her arms and legs	An octopus or cuttlefish
Squat and wrinkled	A prune
Possessed of a large head and skinny body	A hammer
Lazy	A sleeping hobbit
Big-eyed	An insect or anime character
Tolerant	Some kind of creature that lives in a giant vegetable for some reason
Amorphous	A one-celled organism, like an amoeba or paramecium. Oooh! How about a euglena?
Wiry	Some kind of electronic gadget

CHAPTER 2

Would You Just Shoot the Video Already?

If you're going to create a video that showcases or fabricates the blindingly awesome qualities of your precocious munchkin in 90 seconds or less, you need just two things:

1. A bunch of stuff that you can make a video with. We call this "equipment."

2. A charismatic baby who's great on camera. We call this "the baby."

Your Equipment: Get It, Use It

1. Get a camera. Do you have a camera? If so, does it record video? If not, do you have a phone, a laptop, a hat, or anything else that might have a camera attached? You understand, you will need some sort of video recording device to create your video. There's just no way around it. If you have the budget, go to an electronics retailer and ask for advice. Imagine the sales associate's shock—a customer! One who, when asked "Can I help you find something?" doesn't snap back "I'm just looking! Back it up, chump!" Don't worry about finding top-of-the line gadgetry; we're talking about the Internet, a topsy-turvy place where grainy, shaky, amateur cinéma vérité footage is prized above all else. Ease of use trumps everything; you don't want to be fumbling for the Record button when little Lilith is discovering her belly button.

Most sellers of digital recording gear will give you a discount if you explain that you're going to make videos of your kid to share on the Internet. They know that once you hit it big, you'll be back for bigger, better, pro-level equipment. But if you're still a credit card shy of being able to get what you need, try borrowing from a friend, the neighbor's children, or the library. Or perhaps buy a camera, keep the receipt, and then return it when your work is done. This is known in the industry as "Blair Witching it."

2. Use it. Do you know how to use the camera? "Sure," you say, "I just turn it on and hope for the best." Really? Is that how you go through life? You've got a child now, one whose opportunity for Internet fame is shrinking by the second, like a lollipop being licked by Steven Tyler. Put some effort into it and employ these basic strategies:

Don't move the camera. If all those 4 a.m. feedings have given you the shakes, invest in a tripod for your camera or prop the phone or whatever on a pile of booties to steady it. Move the camera as little as possible.

Eliminate extraneous noise. The sound system on your camera is probably crappy, so experiment to figure out how crappy it is. Do some tests, holding the camera at various distances while baby Megan's delightful laughter makes you feel sorry for all the childless single people of the world. Get rid of background noise: close windows and doors, turn off TVs and radios, shush anyone you can't shove out of the room. Shush repeatedly if necessary.

Get close. Shooting from the sidelines is for football highlight reels and the White House press corps. Get that camera right in the thick of the action, so close that your viewers will feel like they are about have apple juice spit all over them.

Create a simple setting. Anything that's not relevant to the cinematic story you're telling needs to get yoinked. If you can find a cleaner, nicer house than yours to shoot in, do it. Consider going to a furniture showroom: you'll find plenty of varied living rooms, kitchens, bedrooms, etc., and there won't be any interior walls in your way. Failing that, invest in one of those portable storage pods that get parked in your yard. Move most of your stuff in there on shooting days. (Or live in the pod and use your house for video only.) Master the aforementioned techniques, and you almost don't even need a baby to create a fantastic Internet baby video. In fact, some say that beloved Internet character Whiz Kid is not really a baby with a tendency to respond to every situation by unleashing a torrent of urine, but is in fact a carefully photographed garden hose. That kind of cinematic craftsmanship takes years to develop, though, and there are no shortcuts.

Cinematic Craftsmanship: 25 Shortcuts That Will Propel Your Baby to the Top of the 'Net

Now that we've covered your equipment needs in exhaustive detail, it's time to put the star in the spotlight. Since it's a given that your baby has the chops to capture the attention of the entire World (Wide Web), the only real challenge is making sure she can turn on the 'zam when you turn on the cam. Now, in a perfect scenario, you would replace your eyes with cameras so that you'd never miss your child's cuteness engine firing on all cylinders. But the limitations of modern surgical techniques make that impossible. So you need to find ways to get that diapered luminary to make with the allure when it's convenient for *you*. To that end, here's a roster of time-tested, doctor-approved* techniques that will all but guarantee a fruitful video session every time.

---

*No.

1. FOOD

Everyone loves to eat. For babies, however, "eat" isn't even in the top five of the things they like to do with food. A bowl of creamed corn might just as well be facial cream; a loaf of bread can easily be transformed into a shoe; a banana might be treated like a sandwich. To your child, a plate of food is a palette from which a universe may be constructed. And then eaten and pooped out. Just provide the raw materials, hit Record, and witness the big bang.

ART

CAN I: Y   N

EAT IT?   ☐   ☒

THROW IT?   ☑   ☐

SMITE MINE   ☑   ☐
ENEMIES ?

2. BALL

Life consists, mostly, of things being thrown at your head.
Babies don't know this, which is why lobbing a plastic or foam
spheroid at them is both hilarious and instructive. Yet they are
quick learners. The typical baby will eventually determine that
if he can't eat it, at least a ball can be thrown, or rolled, at the
nearest enemy.

AMBIENT → CUTENESS

3. LITTLE ANIMALS

Looks aren't everything—except on the Internet, where they are the means by which the world will pass instant judgment. If your wee one possesses not only the gentle and generous personality of a Mother Theresa but also the haggard, cronish *appearance* of Mother Theresa, stack your videos with some ringers: kittens, puppies, ducklings, eaglets, whatever. Your baby will absorb their ambient cuteness as if it was secondhand smoke. Plus, your video will appeal to people who perhaps hate children but love animals (known in the biz as a "crossover hit").

4. LEMON

"Lemon tree, very pretty," the song goes, "and de lemon flower is sweet. But de fruit of de poor lemon is impossible to eat." Truly the lemon is one of nature's meanest jokes: a primary-colored, exquisitely scented fruit—who could blame a baby for putting a piece of it in her mouth? Especially when you hand it to her. And then . . . oh, baby! We have sour-sensitive taste buds on our tongues for a reason.

"WHEN LIFE GIVES YOU LEMONS, HAND THEM TO AN UNSUSPECTING CHILD."

—Siddhartha

5. STUPID DAD

If decades of television, movies, comic strips, stand-up comedy, and other forms of modern-day pop culture have taught us anything, it's this: the idea that a dad can possibly perform any childcare task as well as a mom is ludicrous at best. Nobody ever went bankrupt by giving their audience exactly what it wants! So rather than spotlighting the competence of your baby's daddy, consider a series of videos displaying a haggard dad's failures as he tries to perform the following parenting tasks: change a diaper, climb out of the crib without waking the baby (why did he climb in there in the first place?), cut an umbilical cord (Da-ad! Let the doctor do it!), and so on. Oh, Dad, just go sit in your den and smoke your pipe. Mom can handle this!

6. MIRROR

So there's baby David, living a pretty carefree life with all his basic needs taken care of by one or more slow-witted, clumsy Goliaths. And then one day, he turns a corner and sees *somebody else who looks exactly like him.* Someone who moves when he does and is even wearing the same clothes. Who is this impostor? Is he there to take the baby's place? Why won't he answer the confused tyke's queries? How dare he mock little David like this! How will the baby react—fear, disbelief, rage, panic, delight, sleepiness?

7. FINGER

Why are fingers so fascinating to babies? Is it because they trigger instincts passed down by our arboreal ancestors who had to cling to the nearest tree branch in order to survive? Or do they just like fingers? Whatever the reason, this is one prop that's always within reach. And if your baby's a biter, so much the better.

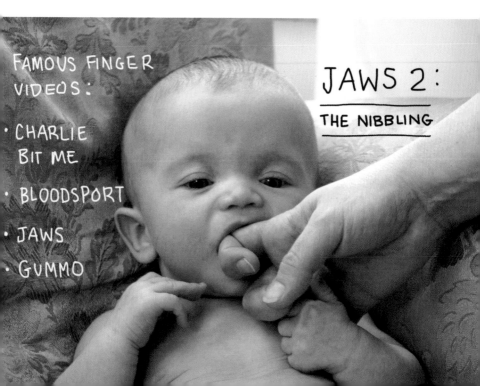

FAMOUS FINGER VIDEOS:

· CHARLIE BIT ME

· BLOODSPORT

· JAWS

· GUMMO

JAWS 2:

THE NIBBLING

8. PIECE OF PAPER

The humble piece of paper has a thousand uses in a baby video.
The tot will enjoy flapping it, crumpling it, gumming it . . . Use
your origami skills to craft a toy for the child, who will immediately
undo hours of work by unfolding the thing and then tearing it up.

Speaking of which, the sight and sound of a piece of paper being torn is *hilarious* to babies.

9. SHADOW

Babies of a certain age start to get cocky, and that's exactly when you bust out this move. Look underneath you—there's a dark creature on the floor, and it's attached to your feet! Now it's following you! Get out of there, run! Hurry!

10. NINJA (ALTERNATELY, ROBOT OR MAN-GILA MONSTER HYBRID)

True drama requires conflict, and in conflict there must always be protagonist and antagonist. So who is the archenemy for your precious darling? Every hero is defined partially by the grandeur of his adversary. So consider a ninja, the deadly mystical warrior of darkness. Perhaps the baby guards an ancient scroll secreted within his crib. Ninja creeps into room. Baby is sound asleep. Ninja moves closer. Baby's eyes flutter open. Ninja tries to blend into the shadows. Baby's hypersensitive hearing detects motion. Zoom in on ninja's eyes. Zoom in on baby's eyes . . . cue fight music. (For Wushu-style stunts, string a doll on invisible wires.)

11. WIND

Do we perceive the wind, or just the effects of the wind? We don't know, philosophers don't know, and your baby sure doesn't know. But open a window or turn on a fan, and suddenly little

Amanda is beset by forces she can't understand: Somebody's touching me but I can't see them? Wha—??? Is it a ghost? Haha, just unplug the fan if things get too intense.

12. BABY'S OWN FOOT

"So there's this thing . . . I guess it's attached to me . . . but it kinda moves around on its own. I try to grab it, see, and then I can feel it being grabbed by me, which is funny, but then it gets away and I want to cry but then I forget about it and then there it is again. Foot!" That's what your baby is thinking in this video.

13. FLOWERPOTS

Where do babies come from? The truth is kind of awful if you think about it. But suppose they just . . . grew out of the soil like flowers? Wouldn't that be nice? These are the kinds of calming, pleasant questions that run through people's minds when they see a baby in a flowerpot. You can take this visual metaphor even further if you want: tape flower petals to the baby's head, pour warm water on the baby from a watering can . . . babies in flowerpots! So cute! Float some plastic bumblebees into the scene.

14. BUG

How can a tiny insect, which has fewer nerve cells than a book of matches has matches, outwit a large-brained organism like your child? Seems impossible . . . and yet it happens every time. Not only will your baby's clumsy failed attempts to catch that little ant, beetle, or tarantula be the stuff of slapstick genius, they'll confirm what so many lonely Internet-video watchers really want to know: the tiniest, most defenseless creatures really can escape the pitiless bludgeoning of a strong bully. You and I both know that isn't true, but let the nerds dream. Let them dream.

15. WATERMELON

There's a reason that the juicy watermelon is known as the "Emperor of Fruits." Whether it's an heirloom variety, like Hobo's Delight, or one of those newfangled square ones, you'll find a million ways to use this adorable edible in your video. How will a baby react when faced with a fruit bigger than he is? Will he climb on it, only to fall asleep on top because doing so took all his energy? What if you cut it open, scoop out most of the fruit, put your baby inside, and let him eat his way out? Have you thought of that? At all?

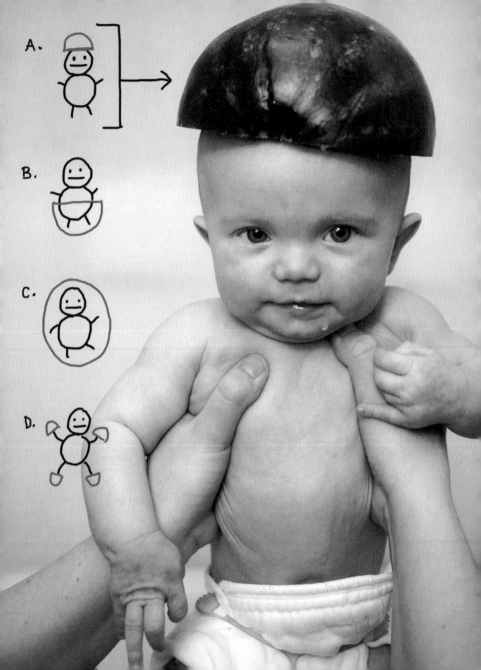

16. FLUFFY WHITE STUFF ON THE FLOOR

What if your baby could lie on top of a cloud? How would that look? Meteorologists and videophiles alike would love the answer to that one! This is a good choice for babies uninterested in physical activity—all they need to do is lie down on something fluffy. That said, don't hesitate to jazz things up with some weather-related props. Maybe a plush lightning bolt? Or a bucket of snowflakes? You kid could become the next Weather Control Baby, whose videos of a maniacal infant seeming to manipulate high pressure systems were an Internet staple not long ago.

17. BUBBLES

Babies figure out pretty fast that gravity is a thing. So present one with these floating orbs and . . . mind blown. The baby may try to catch and destroy the creatures that have offended her sense of reality . . . or she may simply stare or, perhaps, laugh like a gibbering lunatic, unable to process this paradigm shift. This is the baby version of dropping acid or watching a David Lynch film.

18. WINGS

But not angel wings because, come on, we've all seen that. Some hospitals even require babies to wear angel wings to liven up the maternity unit. Be creative! Consider that the type of wings you choose can say lots about your baby's personality. Butterfly wings imply a light-hearted delicate persona. Crow wings suggest a liking for eating food off the floor. Owl wings, intelligence. Airplane wings, rigidity. Bat wings, the ability to see in the dark.

OPTIONS

YES!

YES!

YES!

YES!

NO!!

19. SHOPPING CART

To you, shopping is drudgery. But to your baby, it's an excursion into a magical world, with brightly colored objects everywhere, music filling the air, and happy strangers whose dull lives need lifting by a brief interaction with an innocent child. Imagine how gratefully enchanted the other shoppers will be when they witness your baby pushing grapefruit after grapefruit onto the floor or ripping open a box of elbow macaroni to throw noodles in the air like confetti. Could I get a price check on whimsy? No, Mr. Supermarket Manager, because it's a gift beyond measure.

20. GIANT HANDS

You've seen pictures like this, probably in black and white: somebody's oversized hands holding a teeny little bairn who is usually wrinkly and sleeping. Why are these so popular? Do the hands represent the capricious hands of fate, which can caress a sleeping baby as easily as they can crumple a man's dreams? Are they just big hands for no reason? Anyway, try doing it on video if you know someone whose hands are freakishly large. But it has to be somebody who's good at holding things.

21. SNOWSUIT

In the cold reaches of the far north, Inuit babies climb out of their whalebone-and-seal-sinew cribs in order to wrestle baby walruses. That may sound harsh, especially for the walruses, but the tribes of the arctic circle know that a bit of exercise in the bracingly cold outdoors will help their children grow strong enough to pull a narwhal out of the sea and beat it with its own tusk. (They don't actually do that, but they could.) They also do it because babies in snowsuits are adorable, as well as prone to aggression, which makes them even more adorable. So don't spend winter cooped up indoors making videos of a happy, warm baby by the fire. Bundle that kid up and let him experience the wonders of the deep freeze.

22. CAPE

If your budget allows investment in only one article of baby stage clothing, this is it. Yes, you can put a cape on her and film her exploits foiling crime in the stately metropolis of Babytown. Perhaps a priceless collection of heirloom alphabet blocks has gone missing. Could this be the work of Blockhead, the Cubic Crook? That's all well and good, but it's predictably uncreative.

The truth is, the cape is the most versatile item in a media star's closet. Just change the accessories, and a cape becomes appropriate garb for a night at the opera, or a flamboyant raiment for a circus performance, or a way for a vampire to shield herself from a holy cross. (Though Li'l Bela the Wampire Waby pretty much owns that last bit.)

STEELY RESOLVE →

A CITY IN NEED ↵

HEROIC POSE

SIDEKICKS ↓ ↓

PRO TIP

FOR ADDED EXCITEMENT, LET CHILD ACTUALLY DRIVE.

23. CAR

The lure of the open road is a classic storytelling theme, so by simply placing your baby in an automobile you'll grab people's attention. Where is the baby going, and why does he have only one tiny suitcase? How is he able to reach the steering wheel and work the pedals? Does he know how to operate the GPS? Can the Teddy Bear take over if the baby gets too tired to drive?

24. FAKE BEARD

Don't babies, with their bald heads, wrinkled features, and endless babbling, in fact seem like wizened sages, capable of dispensing universal truths if only they had a grasp of verbal communication? Just place a beard on little Brett and suddenly you've conjured the screen presence of a Zen master. It's a trenchant comment on youth and age. Superimpose some pithy advice on the screen— maybe something from an old Windows Vista commercial. "The wow starts now!" No, that's not good.

25. HORSE HEAD

Used to be every family kept a horse head of some sort around the house. But these days, not so much. Nevertheless, if you're able to acquire one—synthetic most likely, which is fine—you'll quickly find that a horse head has dozens of uses in a compelling baby video. Perhaps you can reenact the famous scene from Francis Ford Coppola's classic film *The Godfather*. Or perform a ritual devoted to Hayagriva, the avatar of Vishnu. Or reproduce some of the more hilarious scenes from the *Mr. Ed* television show. Or simply explore what life might be like for a human baby raised by a centaur. And those are just some of the obvious ideas.

A. BABY HEAD
DIFFERENCES
· ONE IS A HORSE
· CHECK FOR MANE
· BABIES DROOL MORE
B. HORSE HEAD

Putting It All Together

You've got your equipment. You've got your baby. You've got an excellent environment to shoot in: the back seat of a surrey, perhaps, or maybe the showroom of your local aquarium dealer. Your baby is bursting with charisma like a puffball about to pop out a cloud of charm spores. You press your camera's power button with your little finger, and the blinky red light indicates you're recording.

And then, nothing.

You freeze. The moment of creation is here, and you've come up empty. What's wrong? Why can't you spin this straw full of potential into cinematic gold?

Don't sweat it. All that's happened is you've failed, and failed miserably. Why? Because you forgot the most important rule of storytelling: tell a story. If you don't do that, your charismatic infant will never become the next Frances McDormand, even if you achieve Coen brothers–level cinematography.

It is possible, if you're lucky, that a story will present itself before your eyes: Little Kate crawls into the frame, wild-eyed and searching for . . . what? She veers back and forth across the rug, erratic, as if she's following some imperceptible siren song or her inner ear infection has returned. And then, success! Beneath a menagerie of plush circus animals, she finds some cow bones that are perfect for whacking the cat with. And here comes the cat! *Fin.*

SOME STORIES WRITE THEMSELVES.

Most of the time you won't have that kind of dumb luck, unfortunately. But you can plan ahead and develop a kick-ass storyline for your videos by making use of what television writer and producer Dan Harmon calls a "story circle," a cycle of dramatic events. Here's how it works, using two famous Internet babies as examples.

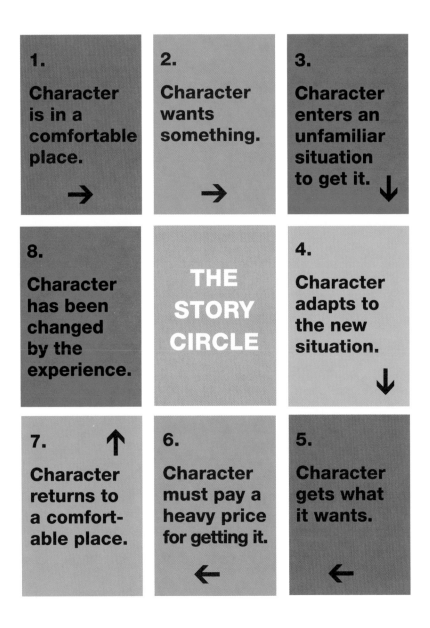

Example 1: Emotion Baby

1. Baby M. is sitting in her high chair.
2. Baby M. wants attention from her mother.
3. Baby M.'s mother begins singing a Rod Stewart song.
4. Horrified at the thought that Rod Stewart may be in the vicinity, Baby M. begins to weep silently.
5. Mother's attention is drawn to Baby M.'s tearful display.
6. Baby M. must endure more of the song.
7. The singing eventually stops; Baby M. relaxes.
8. Will there be more singing? What if next it's "Maggie May"?

Example 2: Charlie the Biter

1. Charlie and his older brother are reclining on the couch.
2. Charlie wishes his brother would quit bugging him.
3. Charlie notices his brother's index finger is close to Charlie's mouth.
4. Charlie bites his brother's index finger, steadily increasing the pressure until his brother shrieks in pain.
5. Charlie's brother stops bugging him.
6. Charlie's brother is crying so loud, Charlie can't hear the TV.
7. Charlie's brother runs away; Charlie has the couch to himself.
8. Charlie now has a taste for human flesh.

Get the idea? Your viewers want to be taken on a journey. Not a long one—about 60–75 seconds should do it. For that length of time, they will lay down their burdens and entrust you to take them somewhere they've never been before, a place called "emotional honesty." Such is the obligation, and the high honor, of the Internet baby video creator. You now have the tools and the techniques . . . and you have the spirit. Deep inside, you always did.

So get out there and make some videos. Make them with all your heart—not only to dial your baby into a future full of privilege, wealth, and prestige, but because the world needs miracles, now more than ever. And you've been blessed with a diaper-clad saint who casts melancholy out of people's hearts the way Saint Patrick cast the snakes out of Ireland. So make your videos, make them until your fingers are raw from pressing Play and your retinas are sore from staring at a Retina display. Let the cynics mock you, let the neighbors call Child Protective Services, let the raccoons feast on the sacks of garbage you had no time to carry to the curb. You live in a world above them all. You are a creator of Internet baby videos. You are the music maker, you are the dreamer of dreams. When you're done, move on to Chapter 3.

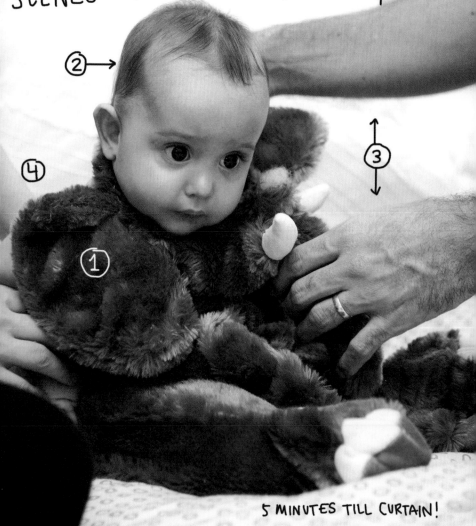

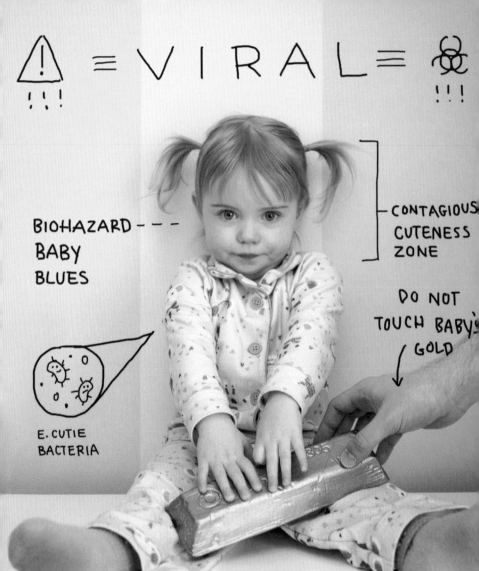

CHAPTER 3

From Bassinet Incubation to Internet Domination

Now we will discuss how to use the Internet to infect the world's bloodstream with the virus of your baby's fame, a virus for which no vaccine will work, not even DPT. The first thing you'll notice when you're done filming (actually, it's "videoing," but that's not a real word no matter what

Spell-checker says) is that your footage isn't very good. Which will send you into an immediate shame spiral as you contemplate your failure to provide your baby with the worldwide adulation he deserves.

Not to worry. The art of film is not in the acting, or the directing, or even in the eating of sandwiches between takes. It's in the *editing*, that magical process by which you eliminate everything that doesn't conform to your vision. You are Michelangelo, chipping away at a block of stone to unlock the magnificent sculpture within. Or Richard Nixon, patiently culling your enemies list until naught remains but loyal anticommunists.

Masterminding Your Masterpiece

Okay, you have hours of footage to work with. And the ideal length for an Internet video is 75 seconds, two minutes tops. So, no problem, right? You might as well give your friend a call and see if she's free for drinks this afternoon.

Hahaha, no. If you want your video to go viral, you can't just stick an .flv extension on any ol' thang and call it a day. You need to sift obsessively through that footage like a grizzled prospector panning for gold in a California canyon. And like that addled prospector, you'll be staring into the saliva-flecked face of madness before you're done. Also buzzards.

Intimidated? Of course you are. But the process seems much easier when you break it down. Every Internet baby video is composed of two types of discrete events:

Moments of cuteness, aka "cutements," or CTMs

**Moments of cringeworthiness,
aka "cringements," or CMTs**

To craft the perfect Internet baby video, simply follow these rules:

CTM > 0	CTM ≥ CMT	CTM / CMT > 1

In other words, you must have at least one cutement in your video, you cannot have more cringements than cutements, and the ratio of cringements to cutements should be as close as possible to, but never equaling, one. Here are some examples:

Cutements (CTM)	Cringements (CMT)
baby yawns and farts at the same time	baby drinks from dog bowl
baby falls asleep on top of sheepdog	baby encounters garter snake in backyard
startled baby makes kung-fu-like arm motions	baby gnaws cigarette—no wait, it's a candy cigarette. No, wait! It's full of sugar!
laughing baby falls over backward onto pillow	baby clocks brother over the head with a See 'n Say
baby offers kitten a lick of her popsicle	baby attempts to nurse from lactating house cat
baby jumps along to exercise video	laughter of baby resembles the gurgling of a Tasmanian devil
jumping baby accidentally hits father in crotch	jumping baby accidentally hits father in crotch

What you need to do now is go through the video you've got, identify the cutements and cringements, and arrange those moments to follow the story you created in Chapter 2. Like this:

Feel-good comedy: CTM + CTM + CTM + CMT + CTM
Thriller: CTM + CMT + CMT + CTM + CTM
Cautionary tale: CMT + CMT + CMT + CMT + (CTM x 5)
Art film: CMT + (CTM x 4) - CMT / CTM x CMT
+ CTM + dream sequence + CTM
Family film: CMT + singing + CMT

SWEETENING THE DEAL

Sometimes—okay, most of the time—even the realest of moments seem fake when viewed on video. That's why you need to heighten the reality, going way past what's real into the realm of the hyperreal. To do that, you can take advantage of the many special "gimmicks" that your editing software makes available to you. Most of these sweeteners fall into two broad categories.

Filters and visual effects. Adding some color or visual flair to your video is a great way to create a signature look. For example:

Use a color filter to match the baby's mood.

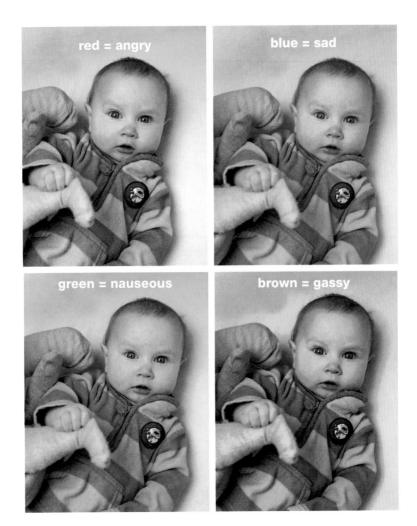

Try an effects filter to add atmosphere.

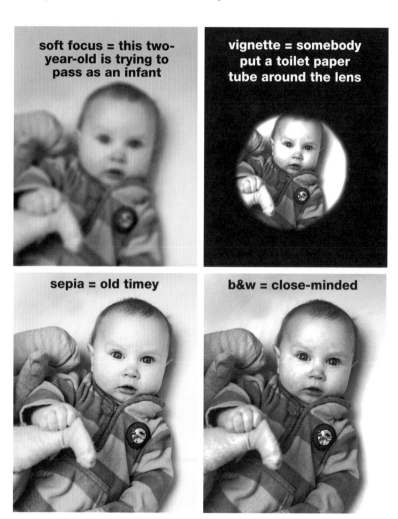

soft focus = this two-year-old is trying to pass as an infant

vignette = somebody put a toilet paper tube around the lens

sepia = old timey

b&w = close-minded

Sound effects. You can't beat a classic sound effect for telling the viewers how they're supposed to feel. Imagine how the same scene—a baby dumping a bowl of cereal, for example—can speak to different aspects of the human experience depending on the accompanying sound effect.

Slide whistle:
"How comical!
The cereal, which
is normally eaten
from a bowl,
is now upon
my tray!"

Wah-wah trumpet:
"Once again, life
has dumped clumpy
misfortune around me.
Can I ever win?"

Boi-oi-oi-oing:
"Despite this setback,
I shall bounce back
with aplomb."

Alien static:
"I shall render
myself seemingly
incompetent to put the
humans at ease."

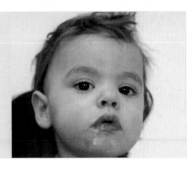

FAMOUS BABY CATCHPHRASES

CHUBS McKENZIE

"That dog isn't getting
my cookie THIS time!"

CANNIBAL KATE

"Babysitters are high in protein!"

PEPÉ

"I'm a little stinker!"

HELIUM HENRY

"I live in a world above you!"

CLOSING THE DEAL

The final moment of your video can make or break the entire experience, just as finding a mouse in your cheesecake can ruin even the finest gourmet meal. (It happens more often than you might think.) So carefully analyze those last few seconds and use them wisely. These are some viable options.

A catchphrase. Some of the greatest Internet baby personalities are as well known for their catchphrases as for anything else. Think of Ice, Ice Baby as he dons his signature sunglasses after throwing an ice cube at another hapless victim: "That was coooool, baby." Or Downton Crabby, the Edwardian Neonate, who always ends his adventures with a hearty "Carson! My diaper is full again!" The best way to implement your child's catchphrase is to display it on the screen at the end of the video. For extra impact, have it spin into place like a whirligig.

A stinger. In the parlance of episodic video, a "stinger" is a surprise final moment after the story seems to be over. Like the envenomed barb of a hornet, the stinger provides a sudden injection of painfully good entertainment. You might finish with a quick glimpse of your baby knocking over the very stack of blocks she took so long to construct, or have a puppy run into the scene and lick the baby's face until they both fall over (a classic baby video motif known as "the ol' slurp and tumble"). Or simply show your baby crawling away from the scene while poignant music plays, like Bill Bixby at the end of each episode of *The Incredible Hulk.*

Mass-Market Your Masterminded Masterpiece

When all is said and done, even the most perfect video is worthless if nobody sees it. Zen koan masters all agree on this point. So now it's time to unleash your creation onto an unsuspecting and soon-to-be-delighted public. You're like a terrorist of love about to blow up the Internet with an explosion of winsomeness. Let's light that fuse!

WHERE TO PUT YOUR VIDEO

You may be wondering, "How can I afford to transmit my precious video to the entire planet? I blew my whole budget on a new case for my iPhone." Well, good news: this part of the scheme is entirely free! Because disseminating homemade videos is the primary function of the Internet, which is funded by the largesse of European socialist nations. All you need to do is upload it to one or more of these notable video-sharing websites:

YouTube: If you have the time and attention span to use only one video-sharing site, this is the one. YouTube is by far the . . . look, can we just drop the writerly convention that you've never heard of this thing? It's embarrassing to both of us. Obviously if you have any interest in the subject matter of this book, you know about YouTube.com. So set up an account, follow the prompts, and upload your video.

The other ones: Watch out, YouTube! Other video sites are on your tail! Seriously, this is the Internet, where once-dominant powers can vanish overnight. Remember AOL, Tripod, Napster, Friendster, MySpace, CompuServe, AltaVista? It's hard to know if any of those were even real. Anyway, don't put all your video eggs in one online basket, or else you may wake up one morning to find that Edward Snowden has put you out of business. For starters, get your vids up on Vimeo, Dailymotion, and Yahoo and then branch out.

KEYWORDING

How are people going to find your awesome baby video when it's but a single diamond in a sea of cubic zirconium? You have two ways around the problem. One is to shrug and walk away, expecting blind luck to do all the heavy lifting. Didn't we talk about this? Are you not serious about making videos of your baby so popular that most people will orient their whole lives around them and therefore secure your child's future as a moneyed titan in a world on the brink of collapse?

Every video site gives you the opportunity to add keywords to your videos. Sometimes they're called "tags," sometimes they're called "findemthings," but it's the same idea: somebody searches for a word or phrase, your video has those words associated with it, and, boom, "Somebody call King Arthur because I have found the holy grail!" But when tagging your masterpiece, don't make the amateur mistake of limiting yourself to words that relate to your video in a *literal* way. Try to think of terms that people would search for even if they're not looking for a video of the world's cutest baby. You're doing those people a favor, because once they see this baby, they'll be forever changed. Here are some ideas to get you started.

Keyword type	Examples
Action words	laughs, enumerates, destroy
Movie and TV titles	*Orange Is the New Black*, *Tron: Legacy*, *MacNeil/Lehrer Report*
Descriptor	mind-numbing, adorkable, cutesplosion
Celebrities and famous names	Rihanna, Louis CK, Eli Whitney
Funny or surprising objects in video	blankie, spark plug, candied persimmon
Not words really	awwwwww, goo-goo, eensy-weensy
Superlatives	cutest, cutest ever, cutest most adorablest smartest unbelievably really funny and cutest
Other famous babies	Prince George, Blue Ivy, Bam-Bam
Current events	Miley Cyrus, Krakatoa, sex scandal

Repetition is the cone that holds the ice cream of Internet fame, so once you've chosen your keywords, use them to create your video's title and description.

Examples of titles that are eye-catching and search engine friendly:

PRINCE GEORGE would be **AMAZED** by this baby's **SINGING** ability. **MIND-NUMBING!**

TORNADO-like appetite of baby **DESTROYS** bowl of **CHICAGO**-style pudding. **SHOCKING!**

ALL THAT! Sleepy baby dozes off to **BEYONCÉ** while her **GRAMMY** knits a new **DRESS**ing gown. **REVEALING!**

FREE IPAD case ruined when **ADORABLE** baby vomits on it during **SUPERBOWL** party. **EXCLUSIVE!**

Monetizing Your Mass-Marketed Masterminded Masterpiece

Okay, it worked! Despite all the doubt and self-sabotage, all the crying, all the baby's crying, all the hours missed from work and time spent shopping for tiny makeup kits, you've pulled it off. You now have an Internet video that the world's eyeballs are tripping all over themselves to see. Time to call the bank and tell them to move your baby's account onto an ark, because there's a deluge of money about to come pouring down!

Where does this moola come from, you ask? You're lucky you didn't raise this issue sooner, when I would have slapped you for your mercenary impertinence. But now, with the big payoff within your grasp, I can reveal that Internet baby videos have, historically, made people rich via three equally important channels. Collectively they are what entrepreneurs know as the Three-Sided Triangle: Advertising, Product Endorsements, and Ancillary Products, or APEAP.

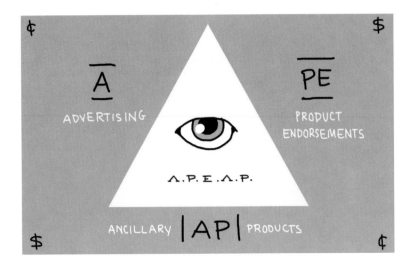

Advertising: It used to be that if you wanted to make money from ads you had to marry a witch, like Darren did on *Bewitched*. But that's the old economy. If you have a YouTube account, you can choose to "monetize" your videos (access this option through your account settings). This means the Y-T will place ads on or near your video, and you get a cut of the revenue. A tiny, tiny, tiny amount. But guess what: the cutest baby on the Internet will pull in more than enough eyeballs to earn her trust fund one penny at a time. Other video sites are getting into the monetization game, too. For example, Vimeo lets you set up a digital "tip jar" so viewers can shell out whatever fee they choose. That's how waitresses and barroom piano players get rich, so why not your child?

Product Endorsements: Direct monetization of your baby videos is a logical first step. But to get *really* wealthy—monocle and top hat wealthy—you'll need to step up your game. Fortunately, once your baby is established as an Internet celebrity, so many people will want your child's endorsement that they'll start offering to invent products for just that purpose. (That's how the Shirley Temple was created.) Try to pick the ones that offer the most amount of coin for the least amount of effort. Some accounts may be able to pay you off in product: diapers, obviously. But one day your child will likely need orthodontia . . . and your orthodontist is likely to be a golfer. "Hello, PGA, don't you think a cute famous baby is just the thing to attract attention to your boring tournaments?"

Ancillary Products: As your child approaches the apex of fame—probably, oh, three to four months into the process—it's time to cut out the middleman. No more taking fees in return for allowing your sweet punkin's likeness to appear on pasta sauce labels and rickety porch furniture. You need to put out some rickety porch furniture of your own—and fast, before little Eric can't fit into his "Darth Baby" onesie anymore and your May the

Forf Be Wiff You video series is all over. The Internet can help! We live in an age of miracles, and you can upload one image to a vendor and have it emblazoned on anything from T-shirts to ashtrays to the business end of a rectal speculum. Try producing small batches of various items and see which ones the fans go nuts for. But do it soon, before that kid's adorable baby face ages into the hideous visage of a 36-month-old has-been.

ironic hipster t-shirt

Whew, that's a lot to take in. As you're juggling all these concerns, don't forget to stop now and then, take a breath, and savor this crazy ride called "supreme fame." You're at the top of the world now, so enjoy the view. And know that from here on out, things will only get better.

right-handed coffee mug

street-legal hot air balloon

novelty miniature tote bag for carrying nickels (shown actual size)

1. MOOSE EARS

2. "NYAH-NYAH" EYES

3. RASPBERRY

4. ESCAPE VEHICLE

FIGURE #20631 G

SIGNS OF REBELLION

CHAPTER 4

Don't Ruin Everything

Okay, you're riding a success bullet aimed squarely between the eyes of eternal fortune. And the game-changing, life-destroying course you're on still seems like the best idea ever, besides which it's too late to turn back now. Or perhaps the sweet wine of worldwide adulation has spoiled into the bitter vinegar of failure—how foolish of you not to read this whole book all the way through before starting your project. Either way, it's important to understand the ways in which the career of an Internet video superstar baby might turn to crap. Read on to learn what mistakes you've likely already made or probably will make, whatever the case may be. Because there are powerful forces conspiring to pull your baby from the lofty heights of the empyrean back down to the squalid earth, where the rest of us conduct the grubby business of mundanity. You can't let that happen.

The Inevitable Drudgeries of Fame

If you've ever glimpsed your favorite celebrity during a candid moment, you may have noticed a certain dead-eyed, blank-faced, haunted expression. That's because fame is as much a burden as it is a boon, one that few can bear without suffering. All true celebrity contains the source of its own destruction, like a tree that's harvested to make axe handles. Here are some pitfalls you'll need to avoid.

Personal-appearance burnout. When the Internet isn't enough, your baby's fans will want to see her in person. To breathe the air she breathes, to wave at her even though she can't yet focus on objects more than three feet away, and to buy batteries at the supermarket or discount pharmacy whose opening she presides over. But catering to all those strangers, with their "Coochie-coochie-coos" and "Over-here-baby-over-here-remember-me-it's-your-grandmas," can be a recipe for crankiness. So book all personal appearances for *after* naptime and hire a baby double to handle the less important venues. Or use a life-size doll dressed in your baby's clothing—nobody will notice. But don't you mix them up!

A plastic body double takes some pressure off your famous baby.

Temper tantrums. A typical baby cries for two main reasons: he's tired or he's hungry. But what about you? Can anyone truly understand the pressures, the challenges, the unique burdens that must be handled by a postmodern filmmaker such as yourself? Frankly, no. So don't hold back. Not only is throwing the occasional fit an important way for you to blow off steam, it will also help babysitters, your spouse, and other lackeys perceive you as a loose canon who should not be angered.

Leeches, moochers, relatives, and other hangers-on. Just as parrots are compelled by nature to sit on the shoulders of pirates, every slacker and goldbrick you know will be irresistibly drawn to the radiance of your baby's renown. Don't let these freeloaders worm their way into your life with their claims of "just wanting to help" and "just needing a place to crash while the landlord sprays for boxelder bugs." Ask them where they were when you needed a place to film your "Baby Dumps Bucket of Motor Oil on a Sofa" video. While they ponder their answer, move to a bigger house without leaving a forwarding address.

Celebrity feuds. Maybe another Internet baby gave yours a pinch while saying hello at the Webby awards. Maybe your baby, just learning to control her limbs, accidentally flipped the bird to Abigail Breslin at a film premiere. However it started, celebrity feuds are great! They keep your swaddled star in the headlines. Just follow two simple rules:

1. Always pick a fight with a celebrity more famous than your baby. Fame follows the rule of osmosis: it flows from a greater concentration to a lesser concentration. You don't want your baby's renown drained away by some second-stringer.

FEUD
STARTER

00573

FUNNY FACE

A THE SQUINT B SHARK C RUDE MOOSE

↑
OTHER
OPTIONS

MAXIMIZE
EXTENSION
↓

2. Bust out a magnanimous apology when the tabloids start losing interest. This makes you the winner: people remember only how a feud ends, not what it was about.

Bad press. You throw a sippy cup onto the floor at a birthday party, you get on a sugar high and run around babbling incoherently, you take off your diaper and fall flat on your face on somebody's front lawn. Then the press gets a hold of it and paints you as some kind of hopped-up lunatic. It can happen to anyone, especially babies. Which is why you need to hedge against this kind of thing with a strong social media platform. Then you can pump your message directly to the fans, unfiltered by some reporter's idea of "facts." To do this your baby must have a Twitter feed, a blog, and a Facebook page. Just don't rely on the baby to keep things updated. As usual, you're going to have to do most of the work.

The Irresistible Advance of Time

Babies grow up so fast! Which is good for the Internet, whose average user has the attention span of a goldfish. Nevertheless, as your baby crawls and then toddles along the path of fame, you'll notice some changes in demeanor. That wide-eyed naif who was once indifferent to the attentions of Dame Fortune will likely become jaded, bored, or even cynical. Here are some things that can happen.

My baby is sick of me. Can it be that the child who's been the center of your world feels like you're crowding her? Typically this doesn't occur until adolescence, but fame accelerates the process. If your baby has a tendency to sigh heavily when you approach, to squirm out of your grip at any opportunity, to raise her arms to complete strangers in the hopes they'll pick her up before you do . . . then yes, your baby is sick of you. Fortunately there's an easy fix. Stare straight into your baby's eyes. Then cover your own face with your hands. Your sudden, paranormal disappearance from view will immediately trigger her instinctive fear of abandonment. Remain hidden from several seconds up to a minute, until the baby's nervous moaning reaches a crescendo, and then drop the facade. Bask in the child's joy at this unexpected but desperately longed-for reunion. Repeat as necessary.

My baby picks fights with siblings. Wait a minute. You mean to say that you embarked on this venture to achieve worldwide fame for your newborn . . . *and you already had children?* Wow. Did it not occur to you that this was a bad idea? Didn't you think about the jealousy, the resentment, the feelings of unworthiness that those kids would experience while you were pouring so much attention into their new baby sib? Is it any wonder they don't get along? Well, I suppose it's too late now. If putting big brother and sister up for adoption is out of the question, consider separating them from the baby by some other means. A boarding school, perhaps, or an extended stay with a maiden aunt who lives in a creepy house out in the country. The important thing is not to let the older kids spoil things for everybody. Plus, maybe they'll have a crazy adventure while they're away.

My baby's aging out of his prime. Well, this has been a concern since day one (i.e., conception). Everyone loves a little baby, but once he starts walking and talking, all some people see is an annoyance. Science has yet to find a way to suspend the aging process, short of placing the baby in a spaceship that flies at the speed of light and therefore no longer experiences the passage of time. Of course, by the time that trip's over, the sun would have burned out long ago and the earth would be a mere legend whispered by the space-dolphins who escaped its destruction eons earlier. Your only option is to try a few tricks of the trade to eke out some extra weeks of filming.

- If your baby's online persona supports it, you could hide the lack of baby fat by adopting a more elaborate costume. El Muchacho Zorro, for example, was able to appear in videos up to age two by switching to a bigger mask and a longer cape. Jungle Jane kept wearing more and more detailed tribal masks to distract from her increasing facility for walking.

- Like other aging actors, your baby might benefit from a slathering of Vaseline on the camera lens. It's a trick that has helped dozens of performers, from Liz Taylor to Broderick Crawford to Johnny Depp. Use about one-eighth inch per baby's age in months past the seventh (off-brand petroleum jelly works just as well and is cheaper, BTW).

- Should the previous tips fail, creative camerawork and editing can take a month or more off your baby's apparent age. Shoot new scenes from a distance and then, for the close-ups, cut to outtakes from prior videos. Film over the baby's shoulder. Keep the baby in shadow for a dramatic and age-hiding effect. Ever notice how Submarine PeeWee, in so many of his videos, was partially hidden by a bulkhead, steam conduit, or periscope handle? That kid was six years old before he stopped posting baby videos, thanks to his parents' willingness to keep rebuilding a bigger and bigger set.

CROP OUT CHILD'S POST-INFANT PHYSIQUE

The Future:
Today Is Tomorrow's Yesterday

Nothing is permanent in this floating world, not even the career of an Internet video baby. But there comes a day when you shut off that webcam for the last time. This can be a confusing time for your baby, who's too young to understand concepts like "overexposure" and "market saturation." Here are some tips for managing your *celeb infante*'s transition into retirement.

Don't indulge the curious. Inevitably, your once-Internet-famous baby will encounter the kind of people who say things like "Didn't you used to be Fall-on-Pile-of-Coats Baby?" This will probably start in daycare and continue past graduate school, so train your child early to respond to such queries with disinterest. Recommend a neutral response like "If you have to ask, then you don't know the answer" or "Pfft. Whatever, weirdo." If pressed, your child should turn the tables on the questioner, saying, "Didn't you use to be . . . oh, I guess I never heard of you."

Maintain high standards. Just because your baby no longer

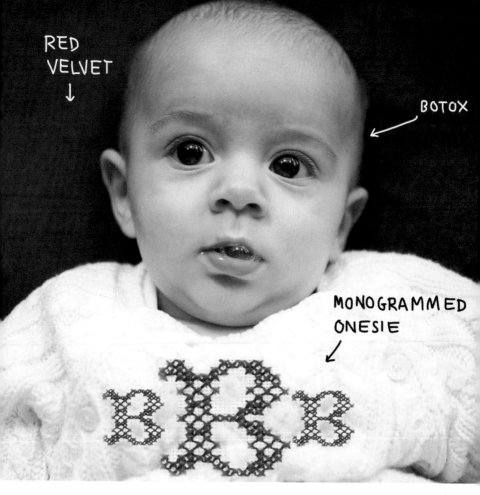

RED
VELVET
↓

BOTOX

MONOGRAMMED
ONESIE
↙

pops up on Dailymotion's channel "Top Ten under Ten Months" is
hardly a reason for him to start thinking he's no better than everyone
else. Because if that were true, why would you have invested so
much time and energy into sharing his remarkable essence with

the world? A good way to preserve his sense of superiority is to monogram just about all of his personal possessions. Shirts. Socks. Alphabet blocks. His favorite brand of graham crackers? You better believe those ought to be monogrammed.

Invest in exotic pets. Most other children, as well as adults, won't be able to relate to the kinds of experiences your superfamous progeny has been through. They won't know what it's like to entertain millions simply by blowing a milk bubble through your nose or understand the unique pressures of growing up without ever having to worry about the slightest discomfort or problem. But your child will need someone to talk to if he isn't going to grow up emotionally kneecapped. Animals make great listeners. And if it's a creature that really has no business being in a domestic setting— a chimp, an anteater, perhaps a rhea— your child will see it as a kindred spirit, another extraordinary being surrounded by uncomprehending dullards.

Indulge, indulge, indulge. Your charming chumbawumba worked hard in that first year of life, so it's only natural that she'll want to take it easy when the curtain goes down. Let her take a year off from preschool and bum around the Chuck E. Cheese if that's what she wants to do. So she's not into fractions, or

doesn't like to spell, or finds tying her shoes a waste of time. You've generated the wherewithal so that others can take care of such trivial things for her, remember? The sooner she learns it's the ordinary suckers who have to contend with the boring and irritating aspects of life, not her, the happier she'll be.

THIS WAY OUT

Okay, time to talk exit strategy. You may be looking forward to it, or you may be dreading it. Maybe you made a complete mess of things and wish you'd never heard the phrase "Must C! kute babee video LOL." Or perhaps, implausibly, you actually pulled it off—but despite your baby's Swiss bank account and the snooty butler who serves you pumpkin spice lattes all year long, you just can't give up the life. One more CNN interview . . . one more appearance on *Ellen* . . . one more BuzzFeed "win" badge. Please?

Nope. We've been over this. Father Time is waiting in the wings like the Apollo Theater clown, about to shove your bundle of joy off the stage with his push broom of chronology. Nothing can stop that broom from executing its bristly task! You have only two options.

Option 1: Bow out gracefully and with dignity. If you play your cards right, you can milk the goodwill of your baby's devotees for years to come by executing a graceful withdrawal from public life. Start by announcing the impending retirement of this beloved Internet personality. Then plan a series of videos bringing the character's story to a dramatic, exquisitely choreographed conclusion, *Breaking Bad* style. As the end nears, your views will skyrocket until the entire World Wide Webbed world tunes in for the final installment. Remember when Jason Jr., the Cereal Killer, produced his final videos? All the speculation over which brand of cereal would be that hockey-masked scamp's next target? And that last clip, when little Jason's supersoakers pop out of his wagon and decimate the box of Franken Berry? Unforgettable.

Leave your fans wanting more, and then vanish from view like Salinger's shyer cousin. That's the wise course. After a few years, with a tentative tweet or thrust or spew or whatever it is that's replaced Twitter by then, you can engender a wave of nostalgia that will enable you to rerelease all those old clips. Imagine, cashing in on the same performances years after the fact without having to create anything new or relevant. It's like you're the Rolling Stones!

Option 2: Go out in a pathetic train wreck of denial and arrogance. Let's face it, this one is more your style. The viewing public thinks *they* can tell *you* when enough's enough? Maybe you should show them that not only is enough not enough, it isn't even too much. Maybe you should continue producing Finger Food Freddy videos despite the fact that Freddy is more than capable of using flatware and even prefers to. Maybe Suddenly Tiffany will keep making her unexpected pop-up visits from behind the sofa even though her eyes betray suspicion that her primary caregiver is subject to a creeping madness. Let the traffic tick down to zero—or even go negative, which means people are hypnotizing themselves to forget the clips they've already watched. Let the comments threads swell with snark, with criticism, with acknowledgments that Bubble Bath Baby can barely fit in the sink anymore.

To crash and burn in this way is to make clear that you follow no one's rules. This is a trait people admire, even as they fill your blog with hate spam. Sure, you risk the mental health of yourself and your child, and you leave yourself open to a negligent parenting lawsuit later in life. But isn't doing it "my way" a reward more precious than any other? Besides, none of the haters can take this away from you:

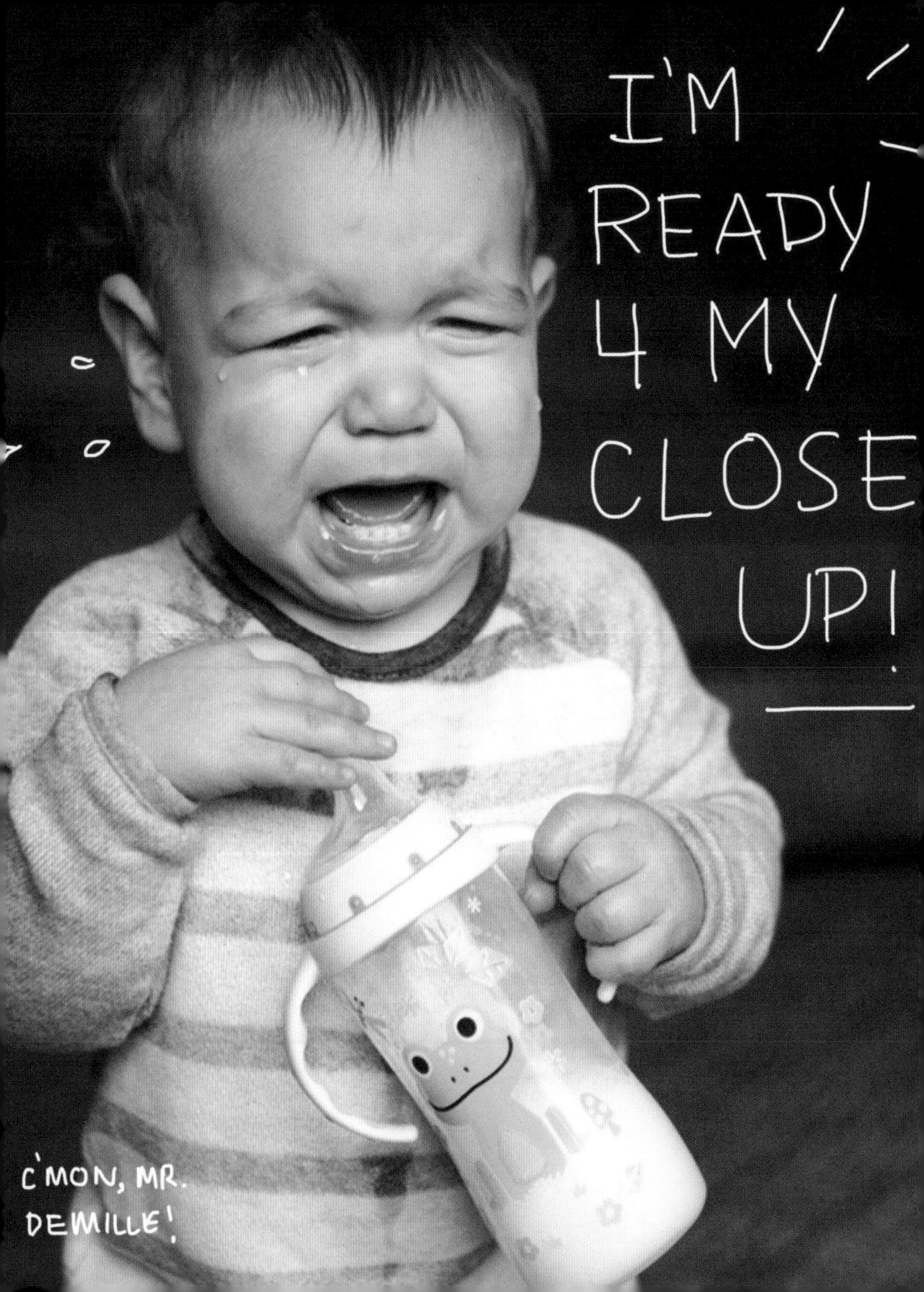
I'M READY 4 MY CLOSE UP!
C'MON, MR. DEMILLE!

For an all-too-brief moment, you grabbed the Internet in both hands and shoved your baby's images down its hyptertexted gullet. You turned the World Wide Web into a giant baby monitor, with your darlin' munchkin making goo-goo noises into the microphone. You stopped the globe itself from spinning so that you could selflessly share your infant's colicky glory with the world. And in doing so, you enriched lives beyond number, bringing joy to millions who otherwise never would have basked in your child's sunlike radiance.

And isn't that what parenting is all about?

Well done, maker of Internet baby videos. Well done.

Acknowledgments

Thank you, Amanda, Jane, Jason, and all of my colleagues at Quirk Books; I wish I was better with words so I could explain how much I enjoy working with all of you. Thanks to Dustin and Doogie for all the visual panache. Thanks to my nephews Charlie, Sam, and Zack for being awesome babies back in the day. Thanks to baby Max and his folks, Rebecca and Josh. Thanks to Susan Pollack for teaching me how to get along with babies. And thanks to my parents for not getting rid of me when a better baby came along (i.e., my sister Suzanne).

—Rick Chillot

I'd like to thank my parents for bringing me into this world, unaware that their son would make a portion of his living photographing babies for this book. Thanks goes out to my older sister; sorry I cried whenever I didn't get my way when we were growing up. I guess I never grew out of that phase (the same one I ended up photographing for several months in early 2014). Thanks to everyone at Quirk for being their usual amount of awesome.

And thanks to the parents who let us include their babies in this book: Jason and Stella, Alicia and Jim, Tara and Seth, Lara and Matt, Rachel and Stefan, Nicole, Julia and Kevin, Jeffrey and Ellen, Laurie and Craig, Emily and Anthony, Kathryn (and Colleen for facilitating that shoot), Neil and Makaylia, Chris and Melissa, Tiffany and Derek, Laura (and Claire for the use of her space), Cammi, Jenny and Jon, Megan and Dave, and Alyssa and Justin. I cannot express how grateful I am for your willingness to allow me into your homes and harass the tiny people in your care.

—Dustin Fenstermacher